T0285970

HOWARD SKEMPTON

50 PRELUDES AND FUGUES

Book 1

OXFORD

for Matthew

50 Preludes and Fugues
Book 1
for organ

HOWARD SKEMPTON

Prelude 1

Commissioned with funds provided by Cameron Marshall.
A recording of Matthew Owens performing *50 Preludes and Fugues for Organ, Book 1* at St George's
Hanover Square is available on the Resonus Classics label, catalogue number RES10336

Duration: *c.*55 mins

Fugue 1

Larghetto

Prelude 2

Adagio

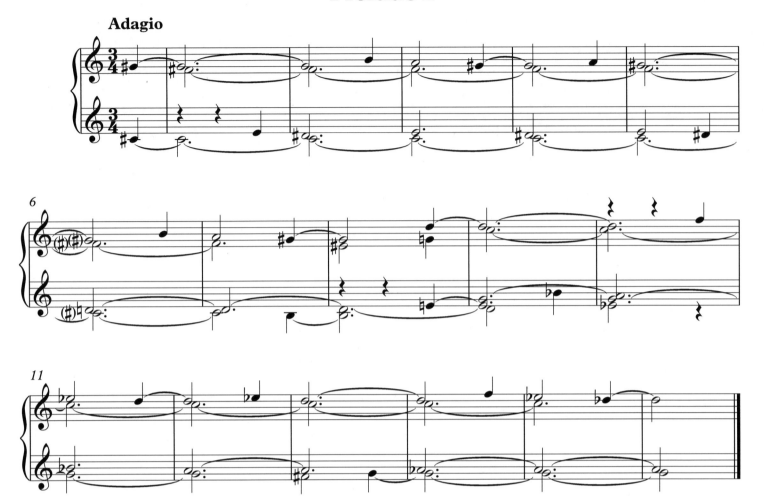

Fugue 2

Prelude 3

Fugue 3

Comodo

Prelude 4

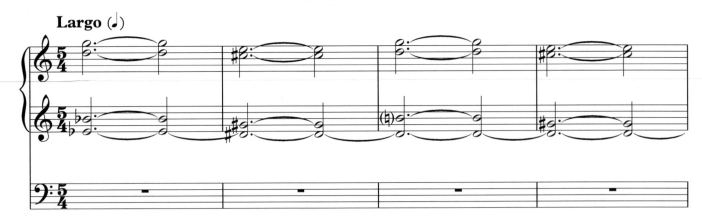

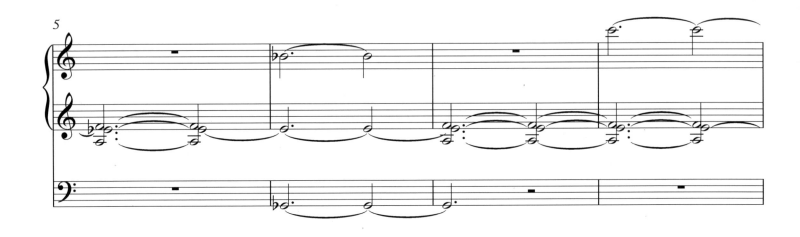

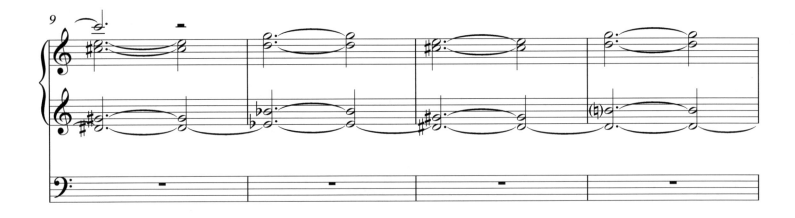

Fugue 4

Larghetto (♩)

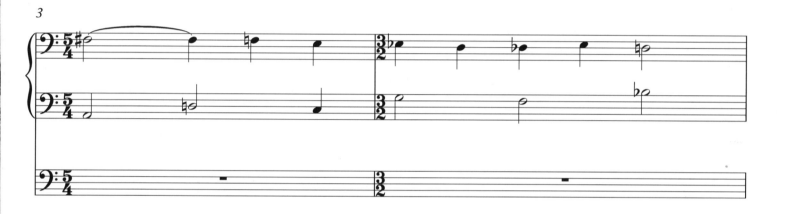

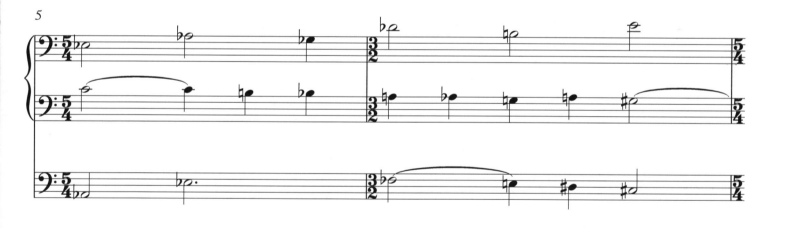

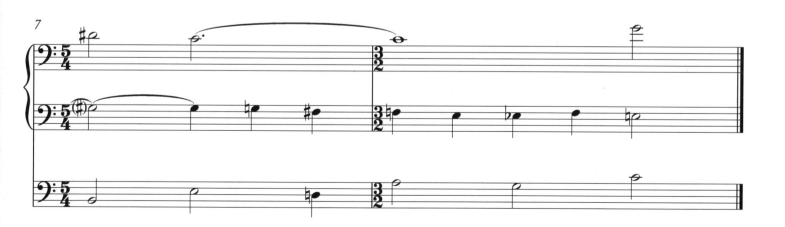

Prelude 5

Fugue 5

Prelude 6

Andante (♩)

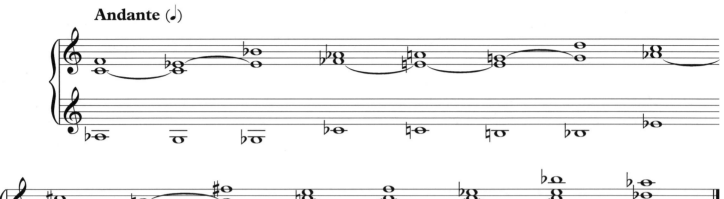

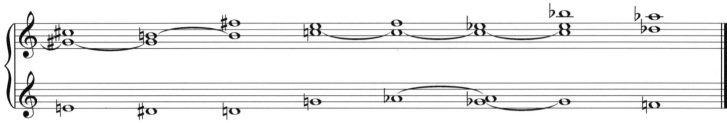

Fugue 6

Larghetto (♩)

Prelude 7

Comodo (♩)

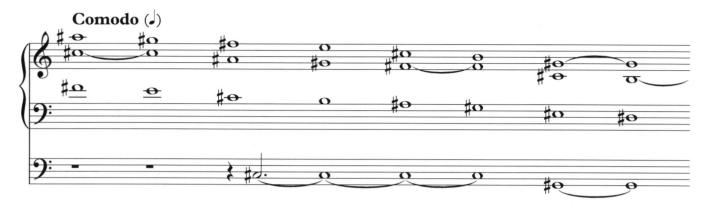

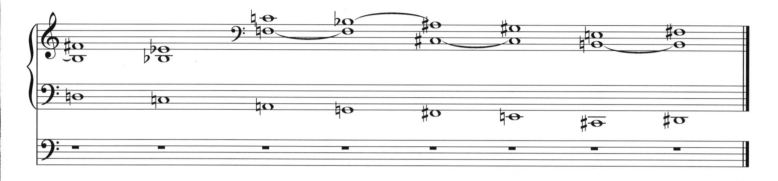

Fugue 7

Andante (♩)

5

9

Prelude 8

Moderato (♩)

Fugue 8

Andante (♩)

Prelude 9

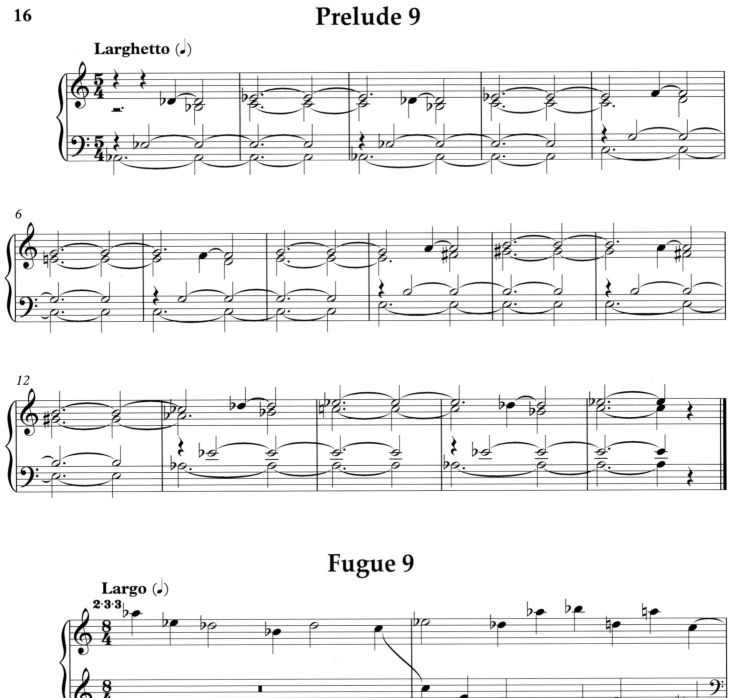

Fugue 9

Prelude 10

Fugue 10

Prelude 11

Fugue 11

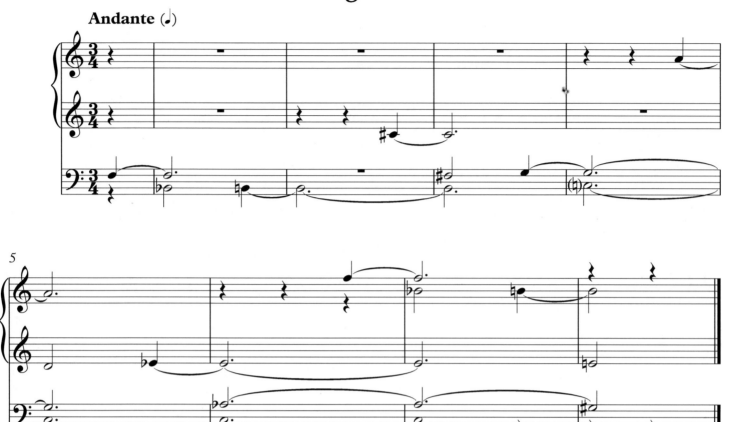

Prelude 12

Fugue 12

Prelude 13

Fugue 13

Prelude 14

Fugue 14

Prelude 15

Fugue 15

Prelude 16

Fugue 16

Largo (♩)

Prelude 17

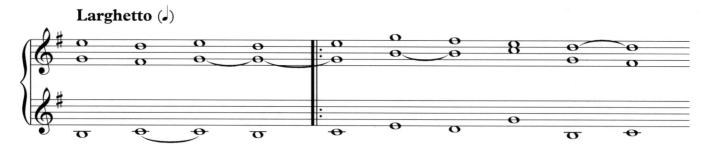

Fugue 17

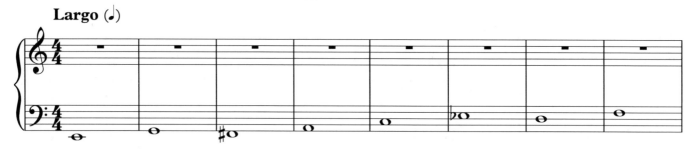

Prelude 18

Larghetto (♩)

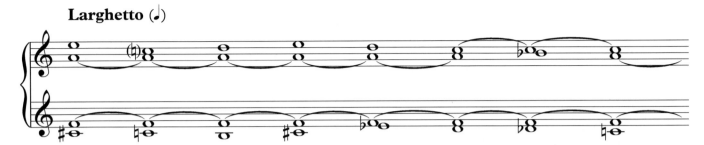

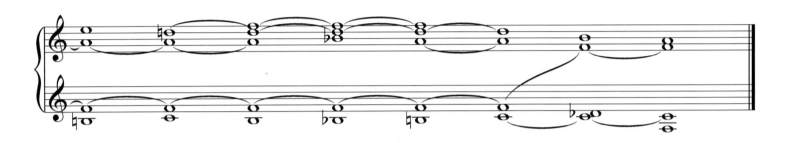

Fugue 18

Comodo (♪)

Prelude 19

Fugue 19

Prelude 20

Larghetto (♩)

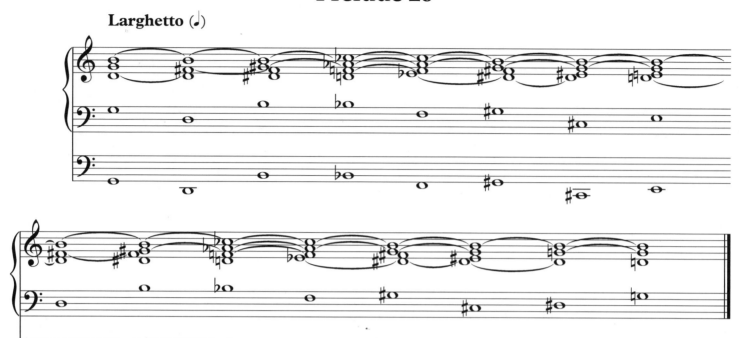

Fugue 20

Comodo (♩)

Prelude 21

Fugue 21

Prelude 22

Fugue 22

Larghetto (♩)

Prelude 23

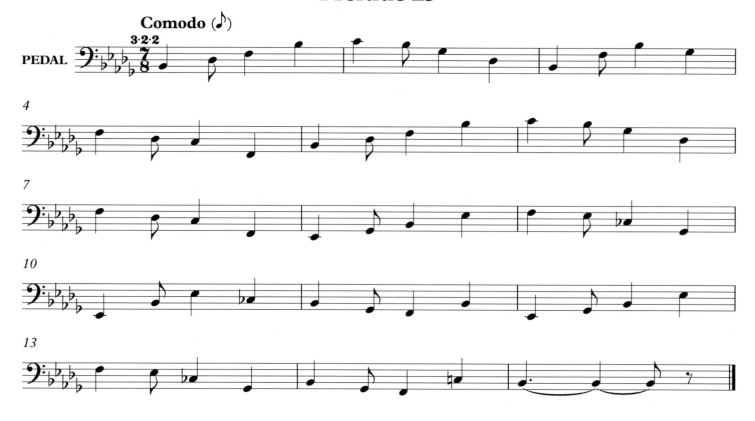

Fugue 23

Prelude 24

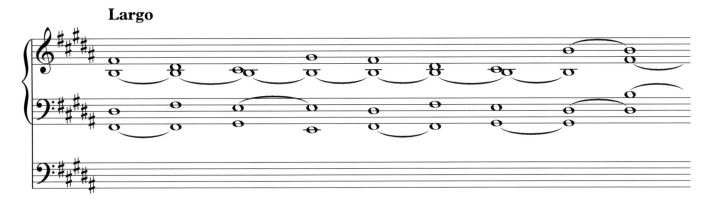

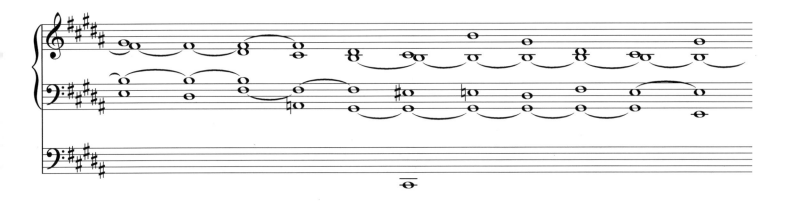

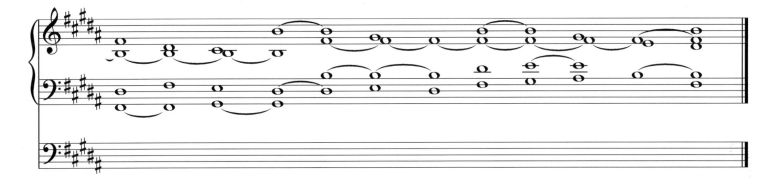

Fugue 24

37

Prelude 25

Andante (♩)

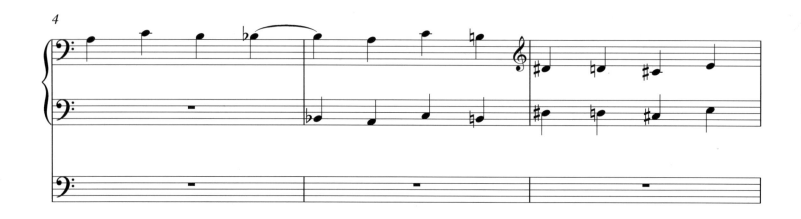

Fugue 25

Comodo (♩.)

Music originated by Julian Elloway

March 2022